Anonymous

Brand book of the Northern New Mexico Stock Growers'

Association:

By-laws and list of members, July 1, 1884

Anonymous

Brand book of the Northern New Mexico Stock Growers' Association:
By-laws and list of members, July 1, 1884

ISBN/EAN: 9783337723620

Printed in Europe, USA, Canada, Australia, Japan

Cover: Foto ©ninafisch / pixelio.de

More available books at **www.hansebooks.com**

BRAND BOOK

OF THE

NORTHERN NEW MEXICO

STOCK GROWERS' ASSOCIATION

BY-LAWS

AND

LIST OF MEMBERS

—————

JULY 1, 1884.

RATON, N. M.:
—THE RATON COMET PRINT.
1884.

OFFICERS.

O. A. HADLEY, President, Raton, N. M.
J. C. LEARY, Sec'y and Treas., Springer, N. M.

VICE-PRESIDENTS.

Don Trinidad Romero, Las Vegas.

M. M. Chase, Cimarron.   J. B. Watrous, Watrous.

EXECUTIVE COMMITTEE.

T. H. Lawrence, Chairman; Jas. P. Campbell.

D. E. Young.	W. J. Parker.
J. S. Holland.	G. W. Stoneroad.
M. Littrell	D. A. Clouthier.
W. B. Stapp.	A. J. Streeter.
John Hill.	Charles Springer.
Oscar McCuistion.	Elijah Johnson.
P. J. Towner.	Francis Clutton.
B. F. Smith.	C. W. Haynes.
Michael Slattery.	J. E. Temple.
Phlem Humphrey.	M. W. Mills.
J. F. Wolford.	T. B. Lane.

Henry Jones.

THE BRANDS IN THIS BOOK ARE ARRANGED ALPHABETICALLY.

MEMBERS OF THE

Northern New Mexico Stockgrowers'

ASSOCIATION.

————

WITH POST OFFICE ADDRESS.

————

James E. Temple	Chico Springs, N. M.
D. C. Pryor	Las Vegas, N. M.
A. J. Howell	Springer, N. M.
N. F. Cook	Springer, N. M.
S. W. Dorsey	Chico Springs, N. M.
W. R. Green	Tr nidad, Colo.
J. S. Holland	Tramperos, N. M.
Francis Clutton	Tequesquite, N. M.
J. W. Dwyer	Raton, N. M.
J. S. Taylor	Weed, Cal.
D. A. Clouthier	Springer, N. M.
T. G. Duncan	Springer, N. M.
Chas. De Foresta	Raton, N. M.
W. O. Van Arsdale	Burton, Kan.
G. A. Bushnell	Tramperos, N. M.
J. F. Woolford	Tramperos, N. M.
J. H. Bosler	Carlisle, Pa.
J. C. Taylor	Springer, N. M.
Simon Davis	Springer, N. M.
Hugh T. Woods	Raton, N. M.
E. C. Griffith	Raton, N. M.
F. M. Darling	Capulin, N. M.
H. M. Porter	Denver, Colo.
M. W. Mills	Springer, N. M.
A. H. Warren	Catalpa, N. M.
E. J. Temple	Boulder, Colo.

Raymond Jenkins_____Kansas City, Mo.
Michael Slattery_____ La Cinta, N. M.
M. M. Chase _____Cimarron, N. M.
J. E. McKown_____Raton, N. M.
Luis A. C. de Baca_____Tequesquite, N. M.
A. G. Shaw_____Raton, N. M.
W. A. Burnett_____Trinidad, Colo.
Richard Steele_____Tequesquite, N. M.
Andrew Morton _____Tequesquite, N. M.
G. W. Stoneroad_____ Cabra Springs, N. M.
S. H. Wells, Jr_____La Cinta, N. M.
Fred J. Hooper_____Red River Springs, N. M.
Frank Huntington_____La Cinta, N. M.
Jas. Campbell_____Watrous, N. M.
Howard Kohn_____La Cinta, N. M.
Arthur Marsland_____Raton, N. M.
Geo. Miller_____Raton, N. M.
T. H. Lawrence_____Las Vegas, N. M.
W. B. Stapp_____Las Vegas, N. M.
J. W. Keller_____ Springer, N. M.
O. A. Hadley_____Raton, N. M.
W. E. Corbett_____Springer, N. M.
W. J. Parker _____Raton, N. M.
R. L. M. Ross_____Raton, N. M.
Garnett Lee_____Raton, N. M.
Chas. Thacker_____Raton, N. M.
J. H. Clouthier _____Springer, N. M.
C. C. Sheppard _____Tequesquite, N. M.
Geo. W. Geer_____Raton, N. M.
Daniel Young_____Capulin, N. M.
Oscar McCuistion_____Raton, N. M.
J. M. Howard_____Capulin, N. M.
J. L Smythe_____Troyburg, N. M.
J. R. Stuyvesant_____Raton, N. M.
A. W. Knox_____Raton, N. M.
A. P. Rogers_____Raton, N. M.
P. J. Towner _____ Chico Springs, N. M.
Charles Springer_____Cimarron, N. M.
G. D. Ford_____Springer, N. M.
M. M. Chase_____Cimarron, N. M.
T. B. Lane_____Raton, N. M.
L. K. Smith_____Chico Springs, N. M.
Frank Noyes_____Raton, N. M.
Louis Hommell_____San Hilario, N. M.
J. M. Gallegos_____San Hilario, N. M.
Hilario Gonzales_____San Hilario, N. M.
E. E. Holmes_____Kansas City, Mo.
J. A. Forbes_____Kansas City, Mo.
M. H. Heck_____Cimarron, N. M.

P. Harsel	Wagon Mound, N. M.
Edward McAlister	Tascosa, Texas.
John Carrico	Springer, N. M.
E. J. Wilcox	Puerto de Luna, N. M.
C. W. Haynes	Las Vegas, N. M.
Chas. Ilfeld	Las Vegas, N. M.
J. R. Timberlake	Liberty, Mo.
L. Walker	La Cinta, N. M.
C. W. Wildenstein	Watrous, N. M.
J. B. Watrous	Watrous, N. M.
Wm. McCartney	Watrous, N. M.
J. C. Leary	Wagon Mound, N. M.
Henry Dold	Las Vegas, N. M.
Hilario Romero	Las Vegas, N. M.
E. Romero	Las Vegas, N. M.
Trinidad Romero	Las Vegas, N. M.
Marion Litterell	Vermejo, N. M.
E. Johnson	Raton, N. M.
Russell Marcy	Raton, N. M.
T. Meloche	Troyburg, N. M.
A. D. Thomson	Montreal, Canada.
D. C. Holcomb	Denver, Colo.
Frank Putnam	Trinidad Colo.
T. F. Maulding	Wagon Mound, N. M.
W. H. Wilcox	" "
Ed Watkins	" "
Samuel Goldsmith	" "
Price Lane	" "
O. K. Chittenden	" "
Frank Cady	Chico Springs, N. M.
John Love	Chico Springs, N. M.
T. Althoff	Las Vegas, N. M.
B. F. Smith	Trinidad, Colo.
J. C. Hill	Chico Springs, N. M.
Henry James	Catalpa, N. M.
O. C. Nelson	Chico Springs, N. M.
R. G. Head	Trinidad, Colo.
W. O. Temple	Chico Springs, N. M.
P. Humphrey	Catalpa, N. M.
Ralph Whistler	Raton, N. M.
N. B. Stoneroad	Cabra Springs, N. M.
G. W. Thompson	Trinidad, Colo.
W. H. Jack	Capulin, N. M.
F. B. Craig	Raton, N. M.
E. Fritzlen	Liberty, N. M.
D. Fritzlen	Liberty, N. M.
S. F. Valdez	Springer, N. M.
N. Valdez	Springer, N. M.
J. M. Valdez	Springer, N. M.

L. S. Rogers................................Fort Bascomb, N. M.
J. S. Elzea................................Wagon Mound, N. M.
M. Cosby..................................Wagon Mound, N. M.
J. M. Bernard.............................Las Vegas, N. M.
M. B. Stockton............................Raton, N. M.
A. Strauss................................Springer, N. M.
A. J. Streeter............................Catalpa, N. M.
J. E. Tompkins............................Springer, N. M.
J. A. Williams............................Springer, N. M.
James Stepp...............................Cimarron, N. M.
Paz Valverde..............................El Moro, Colo.
John B. Garth.............................Wagon Mound, N. M.
C. J. Jones...............................Springer, N. M.
T. M. Michaels............................Springer, N. M.
W. E. Ewing...............................La Cinta, N. M.
H. T. Sinclair............................Wagon Mound, N. M.
Wm. Anderson..............................Trinidad, Colo.
Frank M. Page.............................Puerto de Luna, N. M.
R. Mingus.................................Puerto de Luna, Colo.
J. W. Lynch...............................Las Vegas, N. M.
K. Ritter.................................Red River Springs, N. M.
J. M. Gonzales............................Tequesquite, N. M.
Robt. D. Marshall.........................Watrous, N. M.
J. A. Judd................................Raton, N. M.

Two applicants...
....

BY-LAWS

—OF THE—

NORTHERN NEW MEXICO

STOCK GROWERS' ASSOCIATION.

NAME.

ARTICLE I. The name of this Association shall be the Northern New Mexico Stock Grower's Association.

OBJECT.

ARTICLE II. The Object of this Association is to promote and protect the interest of stock growers and dealers in live stock within the Territory of New Mexico; to detect and prevent the stealing of live stock, and to aid in the enforcement of the stock laws of the Territory.

BOARD OF DIRECTORS.

ARTICLE III. The affairs and concerns of this Association shall be under the management and control of a Board of twenty-nine Directors and the President, the three Vice-Presidents, the Secretary and the Executive Committee shall, by virtue of their offices, be such directors.

OFFICERS.

ARTICLE IV. The officers of this Association shall be a President, three Vice-Presidents, a Secretary, a Treasurer, and an Executive Committee of twenty-four members, in addition to the President, the three Vice-Presidents and the Secretary of the Association, who shall be members ex officio of this Committee. The officers and the Executive Committee shall be elected at each annual meeting of the Association, and shall serve for one year, or until their successors are elected and qualified.

DUTIES OF OFFICERS.

ARTICLE V.

PRESIDENT.

The President shall preside at all meetings of the Association. He shall see that the rules and regulations thereof are enforced, and shall perform such other duties as usually pertain to his office.

VICE-PRESIDENT.

In the absence of the President the senior Vice-President present shall perform the duties of the former, and if the President and all the Vice-Presidents be absent at any meeting, a President pro tempore may be elected.

SECRETARY.

The Secretary shall keep accurate minutes of the proceedings of the Association at its various meetings. He shall keep a roll of members, and shall collect and pay over to the Treasurer all fees, dues and assessments due from members. He shall keep such books of record and account as shall show at all times the exact condition of the affairs of the Association, which books shall at all times be subject to inspection by members of the Executive Committee. He shall draw all orders of the Executive Committee on the Treasurer, and shall make a full report of all the transactions of his office at each annual meeting, and at such other times as the Executive Committee may direct. He shall perform such other duties as usually pertain to his office.

TREASURER.

The Treasurer shall receive from the Secretary all moneys belonging to the Association, and shall disburse the same on orders of the Executive Committee, attested by the Secretary. He shall keep a correct account of all such receipts and disbursements, and shall make a full report of all the transactions of his office at each annual meeting, at such other times as the Executive Committee may direct, and shall produce proper vouchers for all disbursements. He shall turn over all money and other property belonging to the Association in his care to his successor, and shall, if required, give a bond in such sum and with such sureties as the Executive Committee may direct, conditioned for the faithful performance of his duties.

EXECUTIVE COMMITTEE.

The Executive Committee shall have entire control of all the business of the Association during its adjournment. They shall audit all claims and accounts against the Association, and shall order vouchers for proper payments to be drawn by the Secretary on the Treasurer.

They shall have power to make and enforce such rules and regulations in regard to round ups, inspections, detection and prosecution of thieves, and other matters as shall seem to them best, and to do and perform any and all other acts and things which they may deem necessary or proper for the interests of the Association or its members. They shall make a report of their actions at each annual meeting. They shall meet immediately after their election each year and elect a Chairman and Secretary. Meetings of this Committee may be called at any time by the Chairman or Secretary, or by any five members of the Committee upon fifteen day's previous notice in writing mailed to the last known address of each member thereof. Seven members shall constitute a quorum for the transaction of business at any meeting of said Committee.

· MEETINGS.

ARTICLE VI. There shall be an annual meeting of the Association on the first Monday in April of each year in the town of Springer, N. M., at 10 o'clock a. m. Suitable rooms for such meetings to be selected by the Executive Committee. Special meetings may be called by the Executive Committee whenever requested by seven members. Each member is entitled to one vote at all meetings, which vote may be cast in person or by proxy approved by the Executive Committee. Fifteen members shall constitute a quorum for the transaction of business at any meeting. Notice of all meetings of the Association shall be in writing mailed to the last known address of each member at least fifteen days prior to the date of each meeting. The call for a special meeting shall state the object of such meeting.

ORDER OF BUSINESS AT MEETINGS.
1. Calling the roll.
2. Reading minutes of last meeting.
3. Election of new members.
4. Unfinished business.
5. Reports of officers.
6. Reports of committees.
7. Election of officers.
8. Election of executive committee.
9. Election of committees.
10. General business.

VACANCIES.

ARTICLE VII. The Executive Committee is empowered to fill any vacancy that may occur by death or otherwise in their own body and among the officers of the Association.

MEMBERSHIP.

ARTICLE VIII. No person shall be a member of this Association except a *bona fide* owner of horned cattle and horses, or the representative thereof. To become a member of this Association the name of the applicant must be proposed at any regularly called meeting by a member, each proposition to be accompanied by the admission fee hereinafter specified. Such proposition shall be referred to a committee of three members, who may report on the same immediately. A ballot shall then be taken, and three dissenting votes shall reject. All persons admitted members bind themselves to the observance of all by-laws and resolutions of the Association that are now in force or that may hereafter be adopted, on penalty of forfeiture of membership. Membership shall be personal. No firm shall be admitted as such, but any number of partners may become members by election and payment of the admission fee in each case. Any member may be expelled for cause at any meeting of the Association, by a two-thirds vote of all members present.

FEES, DUES AND ASSESSMENTS.

ARTICLE IX. The admission fee shall be $2.50, payable at time of election, and no member shall become a member without such payment. The annual dues shall be $2.50, payable in advance at each annual meeting. Any member failing to pay his dues before the next annual meeting shall cease to be a member. Any member who has been dropped for non-payment of dues or assessments shall, before he can be reinstated, pay to the Secretary all dues and assessments for the period from his last payment to the date of his application for reinstatement, as though he had remained a member. All members shall be subject to assessments not exceeding in the aggregate two cents per head per annum for all cattle, horses and mules, of which each member may, at the time of assessment be the owner or representative. These assessments may be levied at the discretion of the Executive Committee and shall be payable when called for. Failure to pay within sixty days from date of any such assessment shall work a forfeiture of membership. Whenever the Executive Committee shall levy an assessment, the Secretary shall send to each member a written notice showing the number of stock he is assessed upon, the rate per head and the total amount. The Secretary shall also keep a record of all such assessments.

BRANDS AND EAR MARKS.

ARTICLE X. Every member shall report to the Secretary his brands and ear marks, and the Secretary shall keep a record of the same.

APPREHENDING THIEVES.

ARTICLE XI. Whenever it shall come to the knowledge of any member of this Association, that any person or persons are engaged in killing or stealing stock of any kind he shall immedeately report the same to Executive Committee, who shall be empowered to act in such manner as will, if possible, bring the guilty party to justice and recover the stolen property. It shall be the duty of each member to give all the assistance in his power to any other member who may be in pursuit of thieves or stolen stock.

SHARE CERTIFICATE.

ARTICLE XII. In consideration of the payment of his admission fee, one share of the capital stock of the Association shall be issued, fully paid up, to each member, and shall be his certificate of membership. These share certificates shall be numbered and shall be non-transferable. Whenever any person ceases to be a member, his certificate shall be cancelled and called in.

WITHDRAWALS.

ARTICLE XIII. Any member may withdraw from the Association and have his name stricken from the list of members by notifying the Executive Committee and paying all dues up to date of such notice.

RESOLUTIONS.

ARTICLE XIV. All resolutions affecting the standing rules and regulations of the Association that have been or may hereafter be passed by a two-thirds vote of all the members present at any duly constituted meeting of the Association, shall be annexed to these By-Laws and shall have the same force and effect as if incorporated herein.

ARTICLE XV. These By-Laws and the Resolutions hereto annexed shall not be annulled or amended except at an annual meeting, or a special meeting called for that purpose, and then only by a two-thirds vote of all the members present.

RESOLUTIONS.

1. *Resolved,* That it is the unanimous sense of this Association that any man who shall turn out female neat cattle upon the range should place with them, at time of turning loose, not less than four serviceable bulls of improved quality for every one hundred head of female which are two years old or upwards at that time. And, further, that on or before July 1st of each year thereafter, every member shall supply the same proportion of bulls of same usefulness and quality, to all female cattle of above age of which he may then be the owner.

Proved violation of the above shall be a proper subject of complaint, penalty to be decided by a majority of all members of the Association present at any annual meeting.

2. *Resolved*, That no member shall gather cattle on any range not his own, without informing the ranchmen in the neighborhood of his intention and giving them fair opportunity to examine the cattle before driving them away.

3. *Resolved*, That the sense of this meeting be that all members of the Association should each year furnish one good, serviceable bull for each twenty (20) head of heifer calves branded, in addition to those already provided.

AKRON LIVE STOCK COMPANY.

P. O., SPRINGER, N. M.

RANGE—Sweetwater and Ocate.

HORSE BRAND, same as above on left hip.

ADDITIONAL BRAND.

left side.

JESUS G. ABREU.

P. O., SPRINGER, N. M.

RANGE—Rayado.

HORSE BRAND, same as cut, on left hip.

ANDERSON & GRATZ.

P. O., CAPULIN, N. M.

RANGE—Trincherita, Dry Cimarron and Capulin Vega.
ADDITIONAL BRANDS.

△⊕ on left side, slit in right ear tin tag in left.

⊕△ on left side, slit in right ear tin tag in left.

F on left hip, slit in right ear.

A ∈ S on left side, slit in right ear.

K on either side, overslope on both ears.

⊠ on either side, overslope on both ears.

▽ on left side.

HORSE BRAND, same as in cut, on left shoulder.

All calves to be branded same as principal brand, on left
side, slit in right ear.

BUSHNELL BROS.

P. O., TRAMPEROS, MORA CO., N. M.
RANGE—Head of Tramperos, Mora Co., N. M.
ADDITIONAL BRANDS.

NY on right side (kept up).
M on right hip.
L on right side.
GA on left hip.
HORSE BRAND, **GA** or **GA** on left hip.

W. A. BURNETT.

P. O., TRINIDAD, COL.
RANGE—Monte Revuelto, San Miguel Co., N. M.
ADDITIONAL BRANDS.

|+| right side

L on left shoulder, **V** on left hip.
HORSE BRAND, **H** on left hip.

L. D. BERNARD.

J. M. BERNARD, Agent.

P. O., LAS VEGAS, N. M.

RANGE—Trementina, Corazon and Los Conchas.

FLESH MARKS—Left side and some few on left hip.

ADDITIONAL BRANDS.

 on left hip.

HORSE BRAND, **D** on left shoulder or hip.

W. D. BLAKEY & CO.

P. O., TROYBURG, N. M.

RANGE—Teneja and Eagle Tail.

ADDITIONAL BRANDS.

+**W** on right side, Flag on right side.   Also some branded Flag on right hip.   Various ear marks.

All increase branded **HV** on right side.

D. A. CLOUTHIER.

P. O., SPRINGER, N. M.

FLESH MARKS—Some have wattles on left jaw.
HORSE BRAND, **C** left shoulder.

CIRCLE CATTLE COMPANY.

ANDREW MORTON, Manager.

P. O., TEQUESQUITE, N. M.

ADDITIONAL BRANDS.

 on left hip.

The following on left side:

None of which are kept up.

HORSE BRAND, on left hip.

Calves branded as in above cut.

J. H. CLOUTHIER.
P. O, SPRINGER, N. M.
RANGE—Rayodo and Cimarron Rivers and Ocate.
ADDITIONAL BRANDS.

 right thigh or side, also **DJC** left side.

HORSE BRAND, same as cut, on left side.

FRANK K. CADY.
P. O., CHICO SPRINGS, N. M.
RANGE—Dorsey's and Canadian River.
ADDITIONAL BRANDS.
GT on left side.

HORSE BRAND, on left shoulder.

FRANCIS CLUTTON.

P. O., TESQUESQUITE, N. M.

RANGE—Big Lake.
ADDITIONAL BRANDS.
— on left shoulder and ＼ on hip,
|

HORSE BRAND, on left shoulder.

CAMPBELL & AUSTIN.

P. O., WATROUS, MORA CO., N. M.

RANGE—Mora and Lapello Rivers.
ADDITIONAL BRANDS.

 on left hip.

HORSE BRAND, on left shoulder.

N. F. COOK.
P. O., SPRINGER, N. M.
RANGE—Sweetwater and Ocate.

ADDITIONAL BRANDS.

AN on right side ; earmarks, swallowfork left, under half crop right ; both brands kept up.

JOHN CARRICO.
P. O., SPRINGER, N. M.
RANGE—Red Lakes.

HORSE BRAND, **JNO** on left thigh.

CHASE, DAWSON & MAULDING.
P. O., CIMARRON, N. M.
RANGE—Vermejo and Poniel.

Ear Marks on some stock reversed.

ADDITIONAL BRANDS.

All young stock branded "horse-shoe" on left hip and right side.

M. G. CHASE.
P. O., CIMARRON, N. M.
RANGE—Poniel and Vermejo.

Some cattle branded **V4** on left side.

CIMARRON CATTLE COMPANY.

M. M. CHASE, Manager.

P. O., CIMARRON, or LIBERTY, N. M.

RANGE—Foot Staked Plains, San Miguel County.

ADDITIONAL BRANDS.

Some cows have **SIT** on left side
Old cows have different ear marks.
HORSE BRAND, **T** on right shoulder

SIMON DAVIS.

P. O., SPRINGER, N. M.

RANGE—Sweetwater and Ocate.

ADDITIONAL BRANDS.

 on left ribs.

HORSE BRAND—Same as cut.

T. G. DUNCAN.

P. O., LA CINTA, N. M.
RANGE—Mule Springs.
ADDITIONAL BRANDS.

 on left hip.

HORSE BRAND, same as other brand, on left hip.

DAMBMANN CATTLE CO.

F. ALTHOF, Treasurer and General Manager.
P. O., LIBERTY, N. M.
RANGE—Tierra Blanco, San Miguel County, N. M.
ADDITIONAL BRANDS.

AAS AS EⱲ **SOD X4X**

HORSE BRAND, Λ left hip.

CHARLES de FORESTA.
P. O., RATON, COLFAX CO.
RANGE—Sugarite and Red River.

ADDITIONAL BRANDS.

HEH on right side.   Ear mark, underbit right.
T right side, full ear.

HORSE BRAND, on left shoulder.

LUIS A. C. De BACA.
P. O., TEQUESQUITE, N. M.
RANGE—Baca's Ranch, Ute Creek.
FLESH MARKS—Two verugas on the left jaw.

ADDITIONAL BRANDS.

F

HORSE BRAND,

DUBUQUE CATTLE CO.

T. H. LAWRENCE, Manager.

P. O., LAS VEGAS, N. M.

RANGE—Tequesquite, Ute and Tremperson, Arroyas, Colfax and Mora Counties.

ADDITIONAL BRANDS.

OO JH OD ED JOE AD HC ILL MG

All calves branded same as in cut.

HORSE BRAND, ΣX on left hip, T on left hip or shoulder.

F. M. DARLING.

P. O., TROYBURG, N. M.

RANGE—Capulin Vega.

ADDITIONAL BRANDS.

IT on left side.

DELANO & DWYER.

P. O., RATON, N. M.

RANGE—Una de Gato, Chicorico, Red River and Gates' Canon.

ADDITIONAL BRANDS.

HORSE BRAND, on left shoulder.

Some branded / on left hip.

NO on left hip, on left shoulder.

EAGLE TAIL CATTLE CO.

O. A. HADLEY, Manager.

P. O., RATON.

RANGE—Eagle Tail and Tenaja.

HORSE BRAND, Same as cut, on left shoulder.

J. S. ELZEA.

P. O., WAGON MOUND, N. M.

RANGE—Between Red and Mora Rivers and Wagon Mound.

ADDITIONAL BRANDS.

 on right side, on left, and on right side and hip.

HORSE BRAND, on right shoulder.

FORD BROS.

TIM PARISH, Manager.

P. O., TEQUESQUITE.

RANGE—Burro Canon.

ADDITIONAL BRANDS.

HORSE BRAND, left hip or shoulder.

D. G. FRITZLEN.

P. O., LIBERTY, N. M.

RANGE—Tierra Blanca.

ADDITIONAL BRANDS.

HORSE BRAND,

E. C. GRIFFITH.

P. O., RATON, N. M.

RANGE—Sugarite and Red River.

HORSE BRAND, same as cut, on left shoulder.

J. M. GALLEJOS.

P. O., SAN HILARIO, SAN MIGUEL CO., N. M.

RANGE—Carrizo de Pajarito.

ADDITIONAL BRANDS.

FR left ribs.

left ribs and **YP** left hip.

15 left hip.

left ribs.

SD on left hip. **C** left shoulder. **B** ribs. **C** on left hind leg. **M——C** connected on left ribs, and **M** on shoulder. **——** on ribs and **C** on hips.

HORSE BRAND—**50** on left hind leg.

GEO. W. GEER.

P. O., RATON, N. M.

RANGE—Castle Rock, N. M.

HORSE BRAND, **77** on left shoulder.

J. M. GONZALES & BROTHER.
P. O., TEQUESQUITE, N. M.
RANGE—Alamocitas.

ADDITIONAL BRANDS.

FLESH MARK Wattle on left thigh.

Some cattle branded same as above on hip.

HORSE BRAND, same as cattle brand, on left shoulder.

HILARIO GONZALES.
P. O., SAN HILARIO.
RANGE—Pajarito and Tierra Blanca, San Miguel Co.

HORSE BRAND, same as above.

A. GREZELACHOWSKI.
P. O., PUERTO DE LUNA.

HOWARD & CO.
P. O. CAPULIN P. O., COLFAX CO., N. M.

RANGE—Dry Cimarron.

ADDITIONAL BRANDS

 on right side.   Underbit right ear.

 on left hip or side or both.   **22** on left hip.

Increase of these two brands are branded **XYZ**

HORSE BRAND, **XYZ** on left hip.

 on left hip.

FRANK HUNTINGTON.

P. O., La Cinta, San Miguel Co.

RANGE—Rincon de La Cinta, La Cinta Creek.

ADDITIONAL BRANDS.

ZH on left side.

HORSE BRAND, **HL** on left thigh; **ZH** some on lef thigh and some on left shoulder.

FRED. J. HOOPER.

P. O., RED RIVER SPRINGS, N. M.

RANGE—Canadian River.

HORSE BRAND, same as cut.

P. H. HARSEL.

P. O., WAGON MOUND.

RANGE—Vermejo.

ADDITIONAL BRANDS.

SV on right side.

HORSE BRAND, half circle on left shoulder.

M. HECK.

P. O., CIMARRON, N. M.

RANGE—Cimarroncito and Canon Bonito.

ADDITIONAL BRANDS.

MH on left side, and others **MH** on left hip.

HORSE BRAND, **MH** on right hip.

HARRIS & COSBY.

P. O., CIMARRON, N. M.

RANGE—Mora River, Mora Co., and Sweetwater Mesa, Colfax Co.

ADDITIONAL BRANDS.

Some branded **MAT** without bar.

HORSE BRAND, anvil on left shoulder.

J. C. HILL.

P. O., CHICO SPRINGS.

RANGE—Ute Creek and Tramperos.

ADDITIONAL BRANDS.

HB on right side. Increase branded as in cut.

HOMMEL & DORSETT BROS.

P. O., SAN HILARIO, SAN MIGUEL CO., N. M.

RANGE—Canadian Valley.

ADDITIONAL BRANDS.

RIO Cattle of this brand have dewlaps, together, one cut from above down, and the other from below up, making a bow.

HORSE BRAND, **H x D** on left thigh.

ILLINOIS LIVE STOCK CO.

J. S. HOLLAND, Manager.

P. O., TRAMPEROS, N. M.

RANGE—Tramperos.

HORSE BRAND, **iL** on left shoulder.

CHAS. ILFELD.

P. O., LAS VEGAS, N. M.

RANGE—Taibon, near Ft. Sumner, N. M.
HORSE BRAND, same as cattle.

J. A. JUDD & CO.

P. O., RATON, N. M.

RANGE—Sugarite River, Las Animas County, Colorado.
HORSE BRAND, same as cattle, on left hip.

JOHNSON & PARKER.
P. O., RATON, N. M.
RANGE—Johnson's Park.
ADDITIONAL BRANDS.

K̄ ⌒ on right side.

HORSE BRAND, 7̄ on left shoulder.

ELIJAH JOHNSON.
P. O., RATON, N. M.
RANGE—Johnson's Park.
ADDITIONAL BRANDS.

W̄ (TW) on left side and N on left hip, ⌒ on right side

ear mark. Crop and split right and swallowfork left.

C. H. JONES.
P. O., SPRINGER.
RANGE—Moreno Valley.
Underbit the right, hole in the left ear.
HORSE BRAND, **LV** on left shoulder.

A. W. KNOX.
P. O., RATON, N. M.
RANGE—Red River.
ADDITIONAL BRANDS.
F on right side. **K** on right hip.
HORSE BRAND, **XC** on left shoulder.

Ranch horses branded **XC** same shoulder.

J. W. KELLER.

P. O., SPRINGER, N. M.

RANGE—Good Night Trail and Canon Blanco.

HORSE BRAND, ||K on right shoulder.

Y. KOHN & CO.

HOWARD KOHN, Manager.

P. O., LA CINTA, N. M.

RANGE—Arroyo de Las Alamosas.

ADDITIONAL BRANDS.

YK some on right side and some on left.

K on left side.

HORSE BRAND, 4 on left shoulder and some on left leg.

KEARNEY CATTLE CO.

P. O., WAGON MOUND, N. M.

RANGE—Vermejo and Red River, Mora Co., N. M.

ADDITIONAL BRANDS.

all on right side.

HORSE BRAND, on right hip.

PRICE LANE.

P. O., WAGON MOUND, N. M.

RANGE—Southeast of Wagon Mound.

HORSE BRAND, L on right shoulder.

LANE & GRINDLE.

P. O., RATON, N. M.

RANGE—Red River.

Old stock various ear marks.

HORSE BRAND, small **L** on left thigh.

MARION LITTRELL.

P. O., VERMEJO, N. M.

RANGE—Vermejo, Red River and Teneja.

HORSE BRAND, **L** on left shoulder and **X** on left thigh.

J. W. LYNCH.
P. O., LAS VEGAS, N. M.

RANGES—Juan Dios for **LJ** Tecolote for thorough-bred.

ADDITIONAL BRANDS.

 J66S

Various earmarks.

HORSE BRAND, same as cut, on left shoulder.

LOVE & BAKER.
P. O., CHICO SPRINGS, N. M.
RANGE—Palo Blanco and Holkco.

ADDITIONAL BRANDS.

 on left side.

HORSE BRAND, **LB** on left shoulder.

LAKE RANCH CATTLE CO.

D. C. Holcomb, Manager.

P. J. Towner, Foreman.

P. O., CHICO SPRINGS, N. M.

RANGE—Ute Creek, Tramperos, Alamositas, and Carrizo, Mora Co., N. M.

ADDITIONAL BRANDS.

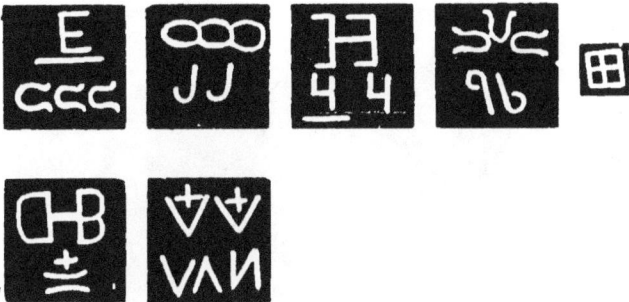

All on left hip or side.

Increase branded as in cut.

HORSE BRAND, same as principal brand. on left hip or shoulder.

LOCOMOTIVE ENG'RS' CATTLE CO.

FRANK B. CRAIG, Gen'l Manager.

P. O., RATON, N. M.

RANGE—Canon Blanco, Mora Co., N. M.

ADDITIONAL BRANDS.

 on right side.

HORSE BRAND, **N** on right shoulder.

WM. McCARTNEY.

J. B. WATROUS, Agent.

P. O., WM. McCARTNEY, Marinette, Wis., or

Jos. B. WATROUS, Watrous, N. M.

RANGE—Canon Largo and neighborhood, San Miguel Co.

HORSE BRAND, **JS** on left shoulder.

JOHN E. McKOWN.

RATON, N. M.

RANGE—Red River and Una de Gato.

ADDITIONAL BRANDS.

DG on left side.

HORSE BRAND, **K** on left hip.

MUSCATINE CATTLE CO.

A. J. Streeter, Superintendent.

P. O., CATALPA, N. M.

RANGE—Dry Cimarron.

ADDITIONAL BRANDS.

HO [brands] Z

HORSE BRAND, same as cut, on left hip.

M. W. MILLS.

P. O., SPRINGER, N. M.

RANGE—Canadian River, Mora County, N. M.

EAR MARKS—Hole in each ear, made with three-quarter inch punch.

HORSE BRAND, same as cut on left shoulder.

MAXWELL CATTLE CO.

M. M. CHASE, Manager.

RANGE—Maxwell Grant, Colfax Co., N. M.

P. O., CIMARRON, N. M.

ADDITIONAL BRANDS.

Some cattle branded same as in cut, on right side and hip.

 on right side.

 on right side, **R** on right thigh.

 on left side, ear mark, crop and split, the left.

KLM on left shoulder, side and hip.

ROBERT J. MARSHALL.

P. O., WATROUS, N. M.

RANGE—Spring Canon, near Largo Canon, south of Mora River.

ADDITIONAL BRANDS.

HORSE BRAND, **VH** on left flank.

THOMAS M. MICHAELS.

P. O., SPRINGER.

RANGE—Sweetwater and Ocate.

ADDITIONAL BRANDS.

 on left ribs.

HORSE BRAND, on left shoulder.

MARSLAND & MILLER.

P. O., RATON, N. M.

RANGE—Chicorica Park.

ADDITIONAL BRANDS.

A or **S** on left side and hip.

HORSE BRAND, same as cut, on left shoulder.

ROBT. MINGUS & CO.

P. O., PUERTO DE LUNA, N. M.

RANGE—Rincon del Alamo Gordo.

ADDITIONAL BRANDS.

 both sides.

HORSE BRAND, same as first additional brand, left hip.

MELOCHE & THOMPSON.
P. O., RATON, N. M.
RANGE—Una de Gato, Kiowa and Palo Blanco.
ADDITIONAL BRANDS.

Ø side and hip, **TK**

HORSE BRAND, **TO** left shoulder.

MARCY & McCUISTION.
P. O., CHICO SPRINGS.
RANGE—Palo Blanco.
ADDITIONAL BRANDS.

Increase same as cut.

on left.

D D̄ D̲ D- -D HH ◫ increase **6u** or **D**

HORSE BRAND, bottle on left shoulder.

FRANK S. NOYES.

P. O., CHICO SPRINGS, COLFAX CO., N. M.

RANGE—Palo Blanco.

Some old stock **K** on left hip only.

HORSE BRAND, **K** on left shoulder.

T. E. OWEN CATTLE CO.

B. F. SMITH, Manager.

P. O., TRINIDAD, COLO.

RANGE—Rock Ranch, Dry Cimarron, Corrumpa Porico, and vicinity.

ADDITIONAL BRANDS.

 JD C ⌐ H

HORSE BRAND, pitchfork on left thigh or shoulder.

THE PRAIRIE CATTLE CO. (Limited.)

R. G. HEAD, Manager, Trinidad, Colo.

PHLEM HUMPHRY, Ranch Supt.

P. O., TRINIDAD, COLO.

RANCH P. O., CATALPA, N. M.

RANGE—Colfax Co., N. M.

ADDITIONAL BRANDS.

7 7 TXT T⊣ J JL 7 I4 77 XT

HI J T̶ ▥ ⰎE ⱯA ⱢL

HORSE BRAND, same as principal brand on left shoulder or thigh.

Arkansas River Division.

WM. WITHERS, Ranch Supt.

RANGE—Bent County, Colo.

ADDITIONAL BRANDS.

⊔H △ ꞁ0ꞁ ⌂ JJ PJ

N C P K

HORSE BRAND, JJ Ⱶ

THE PRAIRIE CATTLE CO. (Limited.)

Canadian River Division.

MAX STEWART, Ranch Supt.

RANGE—Oldham County, Texas.

ADDITIONAL BRANDS.

HORSE BRAND, same as cattle.

W. J. PARKER.

P. O., RATON, N. M.

RANGE—Sugarite and Una de Gato.

ADDITIONAL BRANDS.

HORSE BRAND, **W** on left thigh.

FRANK PUTNAM.

P. O., TRINIDAD, COLO.

RANGE—Red River.

ADDITIONAL BRANDS.

+ left side.

HORSE BRAND, same as cut, on left thigh.

THE PORTSMOUTH CATTLE CO.

E. F. Holmes, Manager.

P. O., KANSAS CITY, MO.

RANGE—Colfax and Mora Co.

ADDITIONAL BRANDS.

left side.

Two dulaps. **P** on steers, and **T⊥** on left side.

HORSE BRAND, some horses **BB**

H. M. PORTER.

P. O., DENVER, COLO.

RANGE—Uraca, Cimarron.

PRYOR BROS.

P. O., SPRINGER, N. M.

RANGE—Southern Colorado and San Miguel Co., N. M.

ADDITIONAL BRANDS.

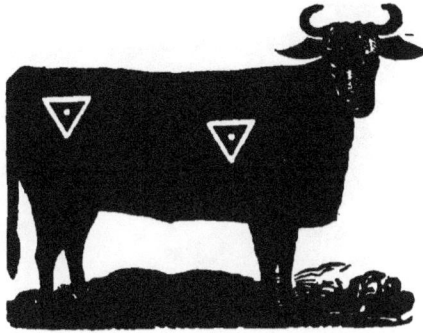

PALO BLANCO CATTLE CO.

S. W. DORSEY, Manager.

P. O., CHICO SPRINGS, N. M.

RANGE—Currumpa, Palo Blanco, Ute Creek, Don Carlos, Holkeo, Chico, Pinavetitos, Senegilla, Carizo, Rafael, Perico, Upper Tramperos and Rio de la Plano.

Thoroughbred Herefords on right side.

Thoroughbred Shorthorns on right hip.

HORSE BRAND, same as above, on right shoulder.

IIII, IIII, IIII, left side or hip.

CS left hip or side.

LRB on left side.

XX on right side.

 left or right side.

T. ROMERO, BROTHER & SON.
P. O., LACINTA, N. M.
RANGES—Atarque Canon, Cuervo Creek, La Garita and Beck Grant.
ADDITIONAL BRANDS.

FLESH MARKS—Veruga below right eye.

RITTER, McALLISTER & GRIFFEN.
RED RIVER SPRINGS, San Miguel Co., N. M.
RANGE—Canadian River and Trujillo.
ADDITIONAL BRANDS.

C left side, C left hip; some single C on left side; some single C left hip. All increase branded same as in cut.

HORSE BRAND, same as principal brand on left shoulder.

RED RIVER CATTLE CO.

Frank Springer, Secretary.

P. O., CIMARRON, N. M.

RANGE—Red River, Colfax and Mora counties, N. M.

ADDITIONAL BRANDS.

Some cattle branded **T** above the bulge of the ribs, mostly on left side.

HORSE BRAND, ⯒ on left shoulder, and ▬ on left hip.

RITTER & McALLISTER.

P. O., RED RIVER SPRINGS, SAN MIGUEL COUNTY, N. M.

RANGE—Canadian River and Trujillo.

ADDITIONAL BRANDS.

Ⓐ left side **ML**

HORSE BRAND, ▬**K** on left hip.

ROBT. L. M. ROSS.

P. O., LA CINTA.

RANGE—Las Alamocitos Creek, San Miguel Co.

ADDITIONAL BRANDS.

kept up.

Not kept up on left side, left hip.

HORSE BRAND, same as cut, on left hip.

L. S. ROGERS.

P. O., LIBERTY, N. M.

RANGE—Monte Rouvelta and south side of Red River.

ADDITIONAL BRANDS.

XLV on left shoulder, side and hip.

HORSE BRAND same as cattle.

A. P. ROGERS.

P. O., TROYBURG, N. M.

RANGE—Laughlin's Peak and Gates Canon.

ADDITIONAL BRANDS.

TIT on right side. **SR** on right side.

HORSE BRAND, **SR** on right thigh.

HENRY T. SINCLAIR.

P. O., WAGON MOUND, N. M.

RANGE—South of Wagon Mound.

ADDITIONAL BRANDS.

T—T on right side. Increase branded same as in cut.

HORSE BRAND, **HT** on left shoulder.

CHARLES SPRINGER.

P. O., CIMARRON, N. M.

RANGE—Cimarron and Uracca Rivers.

ADDITIONAL BRANDS.

Thoroughbred Stock, **CS** on right side.

Some stock branded **B BX** right hip and side.

HORSE BRAND, **CS** on right shoulder.

M. B. STOCKTON.

P. O., RATON, N. M.

RANGE—Red River.

ALBERT G. SHAW.
P. O., RATON, N. M.
RANGE—Sugarite and Red River.
ADDITIONAL BRANDS.

 (IXI) VV

HORSE BRAND, same as cut, on left shoulder, also **W** on left shoulder, and **H** on right shoulder.

RICHARD STEELE.
P. O., TEQUESQUITE.
RANGE—Tequesquite, Ute and Canadian Rivers.
ADDITIONAL BRANDS

DS on left side and on left side.

HORSE BRAND, **DS** on left shoulder.

L. K. SMITH.

P. O., CHICO SPRINGS.

RANGE—Chico and Rita Plains.

ADDITIONAL BRANDS.

T ISI FG   all on left side, or hip.
—X on side. ─╂─ on hip. Ear mark same as cut.
All increase branded same as in cut.

J. L. SMYTHE.

P. O., TROYBURG, N. M.

RANGE—Teneja and Red River.

HORSE BRAND, same as cut, on right thigh.

A. STRAUSS.

P. O., CHAPERITO, SAN MIGUEL CO.. N. M.

RANGE—Rincon del Charco.

SHEPARD & HALL.

P. O., TEQUESQUITE, N. M.

RANGE—Alamositas, Mora County.

ADDITIONAL BRANDS.

ΛVΛ right side and hip, **SS** left side, right side.

This brand is kept up.

HORSE BRAND—**Y** left hip or shoulder.

JAMES M. STEPP.

P. O., CIMARRON, N. M.

RANGE—Cimarron River.

ADDITIONAL BRANDS.

STEP and ▣ on left shoulder, **T** on left side.

HORSE BRAND, ◊| on left shoulder.

W. B. STAPP.

P. O., LAS VEGAS, N. M.

ADDITIONAL BRANDS.

SH on left ribs.

S on jaw, **S** on ribs, **S̄** on thigh.

76 on left rump or hip.

SOUTH & CHITTENDEN.
P. O., WAGON MOUND.
RANGE—Vermejo and Tatoveque.
ADDITIONAL BRANDS.
I6 left hip and side, TIi right hip and side, HH right
hip and side.
HORSE BRAND, T on right shoulder.

STONEROAD BROS.
P. O., CABRA SPRINGS, N. M.
RANGE—The Beck Grant.
HORSE BRAND, 2 on left thigh.

GEO. W. THOMPSON.
P. O., TRINIDAD, COLO.
RANGE—Chaquaque and Trinchera.
HORSE BRAND, box (as above) on left shoulder or hip.

P. J. TOWNER.
P. O.. SPRINGER, N. M.
RANGE—Dorsey Range.
HORSE BRAND, same as cut, on right flank.

JOHN C. TAYLOR.

P. O., SPRINGER, N. M.

RANGE—Red River,

ADDITIONAL BRANDS.

 on left side.

 on right side

HORSE BRAND, $\widehat{\mathbf{J}}$ on left shoulder.

CHAS. THACKER.

P. O., RATON, N. M.

RANGE—Red River, from up Eagle Tail Mountain.

ADDITIONAL BRANDS.

SC on left side.

HORSE BRAND, same as cut on left thigh.

TIMBERLAKE BROS.
WAGON MOUND, N. M.
RANGE—Vermejo and Mora River.
ADDITIONAL BRANDS.

7 I 7 right hip, side or shoulder.

HORSE BRAND, **XA** on right shoulder.

J. E TOMPKINS.
P. O., SPRINGER, N. M.
RANGE—Sweet Water Valley.
ADDITIONAL BRANDS.

T C   on left side.

HORSE BRAND,   on left hip.

DANIEL TROY AND PIEPER.

P. O., TROYBURG, N. M.

RANGE—Capulin, Mesa Larga and Kiowa.

HORSE BRAND, same as cut, on left shoulder.

ED. J. TEMPLE.

P. O., CHICO SPRINGS, N. M.

RANGE—Chico, Rita Plain and Palo Blanco.

ADDITIONAL BRANDS.

xx

J. E. TEMPLE.

P. O., CHICO SPRINGS, N. M.

RANGE--Palo Blanco, Chico and Holkeo.

ADDITIONAL BRANDS.

Z HJT FJT CT

HORSE BRAND, **J** left shoulder, **T** left hip.
Young horses branded **JT** on left hip.

J. S. TAYLOR.

P. O., WEED, CAL.

RANGE--Red River.

ADDITIONAL BRANDS.

O one or both sides.

Z or on left side.

 right side.

All young stock branded on both sides.

HORSE BRAND, **+7** right shoulder.

SANTIAGO F. VALDEZ.
P. O. SPRINGER, N. M., COLFAX CO.

RANGE—Cimarron and Rayado Rivers; Ocate. Sweet-water and La Agueje.

Overslope and underbit left jinglebob on right ear.

Cattle on cut only ear marks.

 Wattle left side of neck and branded only on the hip.

ADDITIONAL BRANDS.

On right or left side.

 Ear mark, two upper bits on each ear; old stock have the wattle and young stock only ear mark.

 same ear mark, branded on the left hip.

HORSE BRAND, same as cattle; all young horses will be branded with the open heart on left hip.

JESUS M. VALDEZ.
P. O., SPRINGER, N. M.
RANGE—Rayado Creek.

FLESH MARKS—Wattle on right side of neck.

HORSE BRAND,-- same as cut.

N. VALDEZ.

P. O., SPRINGER, N. M.

RANGE—Rayado Creek, Colfax Co.

ADDITIONAL BRANDS.

 on left hip, no ear mark, **EV** on left side.

All have wattle on left side of neck.

HORSE BRAND, same as cattle, on left hip.

PAZ VALVERDE.

P. O., SPRINGER, N. M.

RANGE—Ute Creek and Alamositos.

HORSE BRAND, same as above.

WAGON MOUND CATTLE CO.
GARTH & LEARY, Managers.
P. O., WAGON MOUND, MORA CO., N. M.
RANGE—Vermejo.
HORSE BRAND, **BOX** on right shoulder.

WOODBURN & MAULDING. ·
P. O., WAGON MOUND, N. M.
RANGE—Vermejo and Red Rivers.
ADDITIONAL BRANDS.
I O U and **OK** connected, left side, under half crop on left ear.

HORSE BRAND, same as above on left hip.

JOHN A. WILLIAMS.

P. O., SPRINGER, N. M.

RANGE—Sweetwater Valley.

FLESH MARKS—Wattle on right neck; calves ear marked, swallow fork in each ear.

HORSE BRAND, **W** on right shoulder.

WESTERN LAND & CATTLE CO.

P. O., CATALPA, COLFAX CO., N. M.

RANGE—Cimarron.

J. A. FORBES, Managing Director.

Cor. 7th and Delaware sts., Kansas City, Mo.

ADDITIONAL BRANDS.

VI WCC ᎳᎢ —X— ◻F

HORSE BRAND, **IOI** on right or left thigh.

VI on left shoulder or thigh.

W on right hip, Ꭲ on right thigh.

LEWIS WALKER.
P. O., LA CINTA, N. M.
RANGE—Sabinnoco and Largito Arrayo.
ADDITIONAL BRANDS.
Some branded **W** on right side, and grub right ear.
HORSE BRAND, **L** on right shoulder.

JOHN F. WOLFORD.
P. O., TRAMPEROS, N. M.
RANGE—Tramperos, Arroya Nueverto.
ADDITIONAL BRANDS.

 on left side.

TKT /**K--I** left side and hip.

HUGH T. WOODS.
P. O., RATON, N. M.
RANGE—Sugarite and Finch.
ADDITIONAL BRANDS.

W-- on left side.

Ear marks, sharp, each ear, (steers).

HORSE BRAND, same as cut, on left shoulder.

RALPH F. WHISTLER.
P. O., RATON.
RANGE—Sugarite.

HORSE BRAND, **ZIP** on left hip.

WADDINGHAM BELL RANCH.

MICHAEL SLATTERY, Manager.

P. O., LA CINTA, SAN MIGUEL CO., N. M,

RANGE—Montoya Grant.

HORSE BRAND, same as cut, on left shoulder

WADDINGHAM CATTLE ASSOCIATION.

RAYMOND JENKINS, Manager.

P. O., FORT BASCOM, N. M.

RANGE—Canadian River and Ute Creek.

ADDITIONAL BRANDS.

4 on each hip, making **44** when seen from behind.

HORSE BRAND, on shoulder.

W. H. WILLCOX.
P. O., WAGON MOUND.
RANGE—Mora and Red Rivers.

Some cattle branded on right side on account of other
brand.

HORSE BRAND, same as cut, on left hip.

S. B. WATROUS & SON.
P. O., WATROUS, N. M.
RANGE—East of Watrous and north and south of Mora
River.

HORSE BRAND, on left shoulder.

CARL W. WILDENSTEIN.

P. O., WATROUS.

RANGE—Petroso and Pinos Altos, Mora County.

ADDITIONAL BRANDS.

HORSE BRAND, same as cut, on left hip or shoulder.

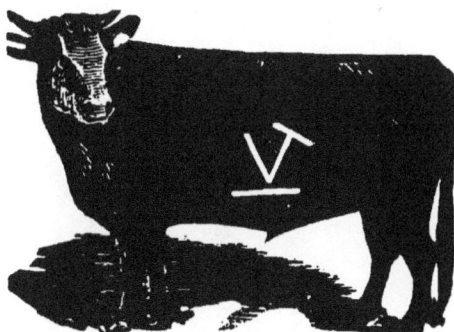

E. WINTER.

P. O., RATON, N. M.

ADDITIONAL BRANDS.

Ŀ on right side.

HORSE BRAND, same as in cut, on left shoulder.

D. E. YOUNG.

P. O., CAPULIN, COLFAX CO., N. M.

RANGE—Fisher Park, head of Dry Cimarron, Oak Canon
and Capulin Country.

ADDITIONAL BRANDS.

left hip. **DAD DAD TAX**

Three last brands all on left side; ear marks as shown in
cut.

HORSE BRAND, **D D** on left shoulder.

ESTABLISHED 1873.

G. O. KECK,
CATTLE SALESMAN.

W. R. CLEMENTS,
HOG SALESMAN.

F. O. FISH, OFFICE.

ANDY J. SNIDER & CO.

——— Nos. 23 & 24 ———

LIVE STOCK EXCHANGE BUILDING,

KANSAS CITY STOCK YARDS.

CONSIGNMENTS SOLICITED.

REFERENCES:

Banks and Business Men of Kansas City.

J. R. STOLLER & CO.

LIVE STOCK

COMMISSION MERCHANTS,

Rooms 6 & 7 Exchange Building,

KANSAS CITY STOCK YARDS.

J. R. STOLLER,	SAM. T. RIAL,
Cattle Salesmen.	

W. H. YANCEY,	JNO. E. HALE,
Hog Salesman.	Office.

WOODS BROTHERS,

LIVE STOCK

Commission Merchants.

UNION STOCK YARDS,

CHICAGO.

EXCHANGE BUILDING,

KANSAS CITY, MO.

Send to us for Advices regarding both
Markets, and for any Information
regarding the state of trade.

R. L. GREER & BROS.

BREEDERS OF

Thoroughbred Short Horn, Hereford and Polled

CATTLE

AULLVILLE,

Lafayette County, Missouri.

(On Lexington and Sedalia Branch of Mo. Pacific R. R.

HAVE ALWAYS ON HAND AND FOR SALE CATTLE
OF THE ABOVE BREEDS.

MAKE SPECIALTY OF CAR LOTS.

FIRST NATIONAL

Convention of Cattlemen

—OF THE—

UNITED STATES,

AT ST. LOUIS,

To be held November 17, 1884.

FOR ANY PARTICULARS

Address

A. T. ATWATER,

Secretary Executive Committee,

Room 20 Singer Building,

ST. LOUIS, MO.

MERMOD, JACCARD & CO.

ST. LOUIS, MO.

THE

Greatest Jewelry House

—— IN THE WEST. ——

WILL MAKE AN ESPECIAL DISPLAY

OF FINE GOODS IN EVERY DEPARTMENT
DURING

The National Convention of Cattlemen,

NOVEMBER 17, 1884.

Stockmen will find us prepared to give them a reception
and show them an enormous number of novelties.

87

MASON S. PETERS.   W. GEE PETERS.

MASON S. PETERS & CO.

LIVE STOCK COMMISSION MERCHANTS

ROBT. MCMURTRA, Cattle Salesman.
GEO. W. NORTON, Office.   ·   **KANSAS CITY, MO.**

REFERENCE: BANK OF KANSAS CITY.

"An examination of the records of the firm of Mason S. Peters & Co. shows beyond a doubt that in a brief period of time they have taken a permanent place in the front rank of live stock commission merchants. Latterly they have secured the services of that stock yards veteran, Mr. ROBT. MCMURTRA, who, as a cattle salesman, is as widely and favorably known as any man in the trade, having pursued that vocation from Boston west, in Buffalo, Chicago and Kansas City."—*Sunday Journal, March* 16, 1884.

W. J. DILLINGHAM, Hog Salesman.   { A. H. NICOL,
W. H. GILL, S. T. GARTH, Cattle Salesmen. {   Office.

DILLINGHAM & GARTH,

❖LIVE✦STOCK❖

COMMISSION MERCHANTS,

Room 3 Exchange Building,

KANSAS CITY STOCK YARDS.

REFERENCES:

Bank of Commerce, Kansas City, Mo.
Wells & Co., Platte City, Mo.
W. F. Norton & Co., Platte City, Mo.
Liberty Saving Association, Liberty, Mo.
Commercial Savings Bank, Liberty, Mo.

Mallory, Son & Co.,

"The Pioneers,"

Live Stock

Commission Merchants,

UNION STOCK YARDS,

CHICAGO, ILL.

———◄——►———

WE SOLICIT CONSIGNMENTS

On this Market, feeling certain of being
able to give every shipper
satisfaction.

HUNTER & EVANS,

✳LIVE✦STOCK✳

Commission ✶ Merchants,

ST. LOUIS, MO.

WE MAKE A SPECIALTY OF THE WORK OF
HANDLING

WESTERN RANGE CATTLE

TO THE ST. LOUIS MARKET.

Address us for quotations and advices.

HUNTER & EVANS.

S. B. WATROUS & SON,

DEALERS IN

CATTLE,

GRAIN,

Flour, Hay & General Merchandise,

WATROUS, MORA CO., N. M.

NATIVE BALED HAY SHIPPED BY THE
CAR LOAD.

E. L. MARTIN & CO.,

DISTILLERS

WHOLESALE DEALERS IN

FINE KENTUCKY WHISKIES,

AND IMPORTERS OF

WINES, GINS, BRANDIES, ALES, ETC.

KANSAS CITY, MO.

The Largest Stock In the West.

WHITE & HOLMES,

Commission Merchants,

EXCHANGE BUILDING.

KANSAS CITY, MO.

REFERENCES:

BANKS, BUSINESS MEN AND OUR CUS-
TOMERS.

W. B. GRIMES DRY GOODS CO.

KANSAS CITY, MISSOURI.

WHOLESALE DEALERS IN

Dry Goods, Notions, Hosiery,

AND FURNISHING GOODS.

Manufacturers of Men's Duck, Denim and Jeans Clothing.

Goods adapted to Ranchmen's Supply Stores a specialty.
Blankets in White, Colored and Mottled from 75 cts. to
$50 per pair. All sizes. Comforts from the cheap-
est to the higest grades. Clocks from $1 to $60
each. Stockmen's Watches, Pocket and
Table Cutlery, large line of Men's Fur-
nishing Goods, Lined and Unlined
Duck, Denim Rubber and Oil
Clothing. Orders solicited.
Lowest prices guaranteed.

W. B. GRIMES DRY GOODS CO.

IRWIN, ALLEN & CO.

EXCHANGE BUILDING,

KANSAS CITY, MO.

Cattle, Hogs and Sheep.

We make it a point to handle Far West cattle to the
benefit of our customers.

MARKET REPORTS FURNISHED.

Call on us when in the city.

IRWIN, ALLEN & CO.

PORTER & CLOUTHIER,

SPRINGER, N. M.

BANKERS BROKERS

FORWARDERS

—AND—

General Commission Merchants.

Ranch Supplies of Every Descrip-
tion carried for Immediate
Delivery.

PRICE LISTS FURNISHED

ON APPLICATION.

C. C. QUINLAN.   S. G. BURNSIDE.
                P. MONTGOMERY.

QUINLAN, MONTGOMERY & CO.,

LIVE STOCK

Commission Merchants.

LIBERAL ADVANCES MADE ON CONSIGNMENTS

Rooms 25 and 26, First Floor, Exchange Building,

KANSAS CITY STOCK YARDS,

KANSAS CITY, MO.

REMOVAL!

SPECIAL ANNOUNCEMENT.

CHEYENNE, WYO., Nov. 20, 1883.

WE have removed our stock of Saddlery Goods, etc., to the elegant three story brick building next door to the First National Bank. Our new quarters are heated by steam, lighted by electric light, elevator, and all modern improvements. With the facilities given by an abundance of room and a large increase to our stock, we now have the FINEST SADDLERY ROOMS IN THE WEST.

We have extended many branches of our business that heretofore we were unable to do for lack of room.

On or about the 20th of December our new Catalogue (now at the lithographers) will be ready for issue, containing cuts of all our new styles of Saddles, and a complete list of outfitting goods. We have added new styles to our Stock Saddles; carry a larger stock of Ranch and Freight Harness, Carriage and Buggy Harness, Chaparejos, made of Calf skin, Angora and Seal skin (the latter are very handsome and durable) all of our own manufacture.

Particular attention is called to our Stockmen's Outfitting Goods, Wall and Wedge Tents, Paulins, Slickers, Belts and Holsters, Feed Bags, Pack Saddles, Horse Blankets, Rain Covers, Drove and Team Whips, Hopples, Reatas, etc.

To Frontier Stores we offer the finest selection of Saddlery Goods of the right kind ever shown in the West. Hickor Stocks and Lashes, San Jose hand made Bits and Spurs (carved and silver inlaid). All styles of Team Whips, Spur Straps, Hat Bands, Saddle Blankets, Cotton Linen, Hair and Rrawhide ropes. Every variety of Riding and Driving Bits. A complete line of English Saddles Bridles, Bits, etc., of our own direct importation. Fine Carriage Robes in Japanese Goat, Esquamaux, Angora, Fox and Wolf Fur.

An elegant line of Plush Robes, Buffalo Robes and Sleigh Bells. Catalogues free upon application.

Very respectfully,

J. S. COLLINS.
JOHN MORRISON. } **J. S. COLLINS & CO.**

---

www.ingramcontent.com/pod-product-compliance
Lightning Source LLC
Chambersburg PA
CBHW021410090426
42742CB00009B/1086